INRI

THE CULT OF
THE VIRGIN

THE CULT OF
THE VIRGIN

OFFERINGS, ORNAMENTS
AND FESTIVALS

MARIE-FRANCE BOYER

WITH 190 ILLUSTRATIONS, 173 IN COLOR

Thames & Hudson

The progressive secularization of modern man has altere[d]
his imagination; a huge residue of mytholog[y]

...e content of his spiritual life, but not broken the mould of
...ngers in the zones that have escaped regimentation.

Mircea Eliade, *Images et symboles*, Paris, 1952

FOR MY DAUGHTER MARINE, ANOTHER STORY, THIS TIME ABOUT

GODDESSES, FAIRIES, QUEENS, MOTHERS AND SONS.

WITH LOVE AND TEARS, MAGIC AND FASHION, SEQUINS, LACE,

JEWELS AND DREAMS.

DESIGNED BY MICHAEL TIGHE

Translated from the French by Jane Brenton

© 2000 Thames & Hudson Ltd, London

First published in hardcover in the United States of America in 2000 by Thames & Hudson Inc., 500 Fifth Avenue, New York, New York 10110

Library of Congress Catalog Card Number 99-66192
ISBN 0-500-01988-6

Printed and bound in Singapore by Tien Wah Press

Half-title: votive offering, paste; France, nineteenth century.
Page 2: Mater Dolorosa, surrounded with ex-votos; chromolithograph. Mount Calvary, Jerusalem, 1872.
Title page: The Virgin of Guadalupe drinking coffee with the goddess Kali, with an image of
Our Lady of Czestochowa. Home altar painting, New Mexico, 1995.
Pages 4–5: Procession of El Rocío, Spain.
This page, background: detail of robe for La Macarena, Seville.

CONTENTS

I grew up in Catholic Brittany during the 1950s, when people still believed in fairies.... Ex-voto boats hung in the chapels, the smell of hot wax lingering beneath them. Velvet banners, starched headdresses moved in procession through fields of ripe grain. There were baskets of rose petals.... I have kept a taste for ritual ever since, whether the Orthodox rites of Kiev or Jain ceremonies in Delhi.

As we move into the twenty-first century, the Virgin Mary remains as much of a cult figure as ever. Millions of the faithful flock to pray to her, in crowds the size you might expect to see at a rock concert or political rally. Their signs of devotion are the most extravagant and the most kitsch, and yet absurdly moving. To some the phenomenon is no more than superstition and idolatry, to others a proof of love and shared human warmth; perhaps it is the manifestation of a collective unconscious yearning for

PREFACE

something beyond. The great Marian images are found everywhere from Sicily to Russia, Andalusia to Ireland, Peru to Belgium, even in India and Indonesia. In France, Our Lady of Lourdes attracts over five million visitors every year, while the Virgin of Guadalupe in Mexico attracts twice that number, and Our Lady of Czestochowa in Poland draws a minimum of five thousand a week. The strangest and most venerated of the images of Mary are undoubtedly the so-called black Virgins.

The Gospels offer little in the way of descriptions of the Virgin, and the Church holds back, responding passively to a huge groundswell of popular emotion even the Reformation could not contain. While it does not condemn the miracles, the Church rarely officially recognizes them. In vain it exhorts the faithful to an interiorization and an austerity judged more in keeping with the expression of religious faith.

Pages 8–9: jewels of the seventeenth and eighteenth centuries sewn on to a robe worn by the Virgin of Czestochowa, Poland.

Page 11: Nuestra Señora de Triana, Seville, patron saint of sailors, homosexuals and gypsies.

Left: The 'miraculous' veil of Mary of Nazareth in Chartres Cathedral, a ninth-century offering by Charlemagne's son. The relic survived a terrible fire, proof, it was said, of its 'imperishability'. Because of the apparent miracle, the cathedral was rebuilt in the twelfth century. Like the Shroud of Turin, the veil has been subjected in the twentieth century to scientific analysis, which places its origin in Palestine in the first century AD.

Opposite above: Cybele, originally from Anatolia; below: Isis of Egypt and Diana of Ephesus.

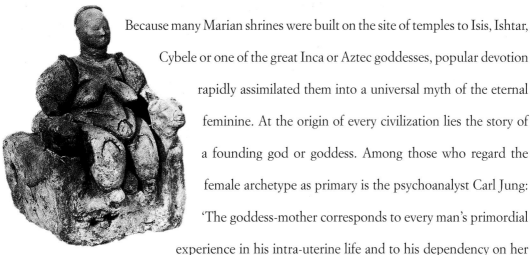

Because many Marian shrines were built on the site of temples to Isis, Ishtar, Cybele or one of the great Inca or Aztec goddesses, popular devotion rapidly assimilated them into a universal myth of the eternal feminine. At the origin of every civilization lies the story of a founding god or goddess. Among those who regard the female archetype as primary is the psychoanalyst Carl Jung: 'The goddess-mother corresponds to every man's primordial experience in his intra-uterine life and to his dependency on her fostering and protective function in early infancy.' Which of course introduces in its turn the concept of the good, bad or ambivalent goddess-mother.

Christians sought to strip Mary of all the destructive, perverse or sexual characteristics associated with the ancient divinities, so creating an indistinct figure calculated to annoy twentieth-century feminists such as Simone de Beauvoir or Marina Warner. But the imagination of the devout was very power-ful and creative. According to the different periods, countries or circumstances in which they lived, believers perpetually reinvented the image of the virtual personality that is the Virgin Mary. Queen or fairy, sorrowing mother, radiant mother, pubescent child, modest, proud, black, yellow or brown, they devised a Virgin to meet all the desires and supplications of the faithful, even the wildest. Thus we have a Virgin who cures stammering, another who stops volcanoes erupting, one who protects bikers, another who resuscitates babies. As Mircea Eliade points out, 'It is the image embodying a whole set of meanings that becomes the true image.'

The little information we have about Mary is contained in the gospels of the four Evangelists written towards the end of the first century AD. Popularized during the second century AD as Christianity developed, these accounts say nothing of her face or appearance, but simply record episodes in her life, such as the Annunciation and the Visitation, specific incidents in the childhood of Jesus in which she played a part, and her presence at the Passion. While we cannot know what she looked like, presumably it was no different from any other young woman married to a Middle Eastern carpenter, caring for her son in a small village in Judaea. From the apocryphal gospels and from oral tradition, we learn other details – for example, that the Virgin went to live with St John in Ephesus, where she died ten or twelve years after Jesus Christ, in AD 40 or 42. In the early years of Christianity we find no visual representa-

FIRST FACES

tions of Christ, his mother or the apostles. The Jewish tradition permitted no images, although other religions of the time made statues of their gods for temple and home worship. Not until the second or third century AD did the first mosaics and murals appear in which Christ and the Virgin were depicted. These were the early icons. A persistent legend had it that St Luke painted Mary and her son in the first century AD, resulting in a flood of icons supposedly by the hand of St Luke. It fell finally to St Augustine to put paid to the legend. By the time of the Council of Ephesus in 431, the cult of the Virgin Mary had already taken strong hold, and the official proclamation that she was the Mother of God, *theotokos*, marked the true beginning of the Marian cult. The first holy image of the Virgin is said to have been discovered in Nazareth at about this time by Eudocia, wife of the Byzantine emperor,

Preceding page: one of the earliest
known representations of the Virgin
Mary, catacombs of Petrus and
Marcellianus, Rome, third century.
Left: detail from the painting of
the Mother of God, monastery
of St Catherine of Sinai, encaustic
on wood, sixth century.
Opposite: the miraculous icon of
Vladimir, Moscow, twelfth century,
originally from Constantinople.
Below: the same icon, covered in
silver, precious stones and baroque

pearls. 'Covers' of this sort were a
thirteenth-century invention. They
could consist of a simple frame, or
they could mask the whole picture.
This example is an *oklad*, here
surmounted by the traditional
Russian headdress or *kokochnik*.
Fabergé, jeweler to the Tsars, used
to make great quantities of them.
They were regarded as reliquaries,
protecting the icons as well as
showing them to advantage.

The dark,
enigmatic features
of the Virgin, with
slash marks; Jasna
Góra monastery,
Czestochowa,
Poland, fourteenth
century.

18

Theodosius II – it was of *Theotokos Hodegetria* (the Mother of God pointing the way), and said to be by St Luke. Eudocia was a passionate collector of everything to do with the mother of Jesus. She sent this icon to her sister-in-law Pulcheria, who gave it to the church at Blachernae in Constantinople. No sooner was it installed than people began to attribute to it a series of miracles, and it was the object of intense devotion up to the fifteenth century and the fall of Constantinople.

Around the sixth century it was copied in the form of Our Lady of the Snows, now in Santa Maria Maggiore in Rome. During a particularly disastrous epidemic of the plague, Pope Gregory I had it carried in procession through the city. An angel appeared and the epidemic ceased. The pope needed no further proof of the icon's powers and sent a copy to Spain; it is the origin of all the versions of Our Lady of Guadalupe. Between the seventh and fifteenth centuries, icons of the Virgin found their way into convents, churches, chapels and private homes all over Europe. As the tally of miracles mounted, so the emotional temperature rose, and the veneration of these icons began to rival the cult of holy relics. It was said that when unbelievers tried to destroy one particular icon, it began to bleed: these holy images, just like relics, were regarded not as mere representations but as real in themselves.

The painting of the Virgin of Czestochowa in Poland is one of the most famous, with more than a million visitors every year. Supposedly discovered by St Helena in Jerusalem, still attributed today to St Luke and said to be painted on three pieces of cypress wood, it was hidden from the iconoclasts in Constantinople until presented to the Polish prince St Ladislaus in the fourteenth century – now reckoned as the date of its execution. When the royal palace was attacked by Tartars, the figure of the Virgin was pierced 'in the neck' by an arrow, and the prince determined to remove it

This page and opposite: robe embroidered with coral, turquoises and pearls, worn by the Virgin of Czestochowa. Like icon covers, these robes, of every date and value, were placed directly on the surface of the painting, and ornamented with many gifts from the faithful. Since the Virgin arrived in Czestochowa in the fourteenth century, offerings have included thousands of diamonds and rubies, hundreds of pearls, and dozens of emeralds and sapphires. To these precious stones were added wedding rings and many other pieces of jewelry – brooches, crosses, necklaces – in seventeenth- and eighteenth-century settings, today constituting a veritable jewelry museum.

to the safety of his birthplace. On the way there he stayed at Czestochowa, and left the icon overnight in a little chapel. When he tried to continue his journey, the horses refused to move, and the Prince realized that the Virgin had 'chosen' to remain in Czestochowa. In the course of many subsequent invasions, the icon has been successively stolen and recovered, damaged, slashed by heretics and reduced to fragments. Through all its restorations, the Virgin has retained the scars which, in the eyes of the Polish people, reflect the condition of their ravaged country. Her image crowned and decked with votive jewels, the black-faced Virgin of Czestochowa is also exceptionally well painted, adding to her mysterious power: the unfathomable gaze lends itself to a variety of interpretations. Silent in the dim candlelight, ornamented with gold, the icon imposes its presence, conveying a message beyond words.

At the time when icons of the Virgin were first in circulation, another representation of Mary began to appear in the frescoes of the Roman catacombs, showing her seated on a throne, regal and hieratic, holding the Child on her knee, like the *Sedes Sapientiae* – the embodiment of the wisdom of God – of the Auvergne in south-western France. This relates to images of Cybele, who originated in Anatolia and reached Constantinople in the sixth century BC. In Rome, where she was enthroned as 'mother of the gods', the orgiastic rituals held by her eunuch priests, involving trances and castrations, were eventually banned. What these figures both retained in common was chastity, and the loss of a son who came back to life in the spring as a symbol of renewal.

Opposite: one of eight hundred copies of the Virgin of Czestochowa that has miraculous powers; since 1954 it has been carried from house to house; Bochnia, Poland, sixteenth century. *Top right*: Our Lady with Bowed Head, Vienna, seventeenth century, much decorated with crucifixes, as too is the painting by Sassoferrato (*bottom right*), church of Santa Maria Formosa, Venice, sixteenth century. *Double page overleaf*: detail of a robe worn by the Virgin of Czestochowa, with seventeenth- and eighteenth-century wedding rings and jewelry.

U. L. Frau mit dem geneigten Haupte.
O Mutter, Dein geneigtes Haupt
Sagt milde „Ja" auf meine Bitten
Und neigt sich tröstend mir herab.
Wenn ich gekämpft, wenn ich gelitten.

23

Her baby clasped to her cheek, or against her heart, on her knee, in his cradle at her feet, in the bed where she has given birth, or clutched tightly to her breast, the Virgin Mary frequently assumes the time-honoured role of the 'good mother', as the people of Marseilles called her. It is one of the happiest images of the Virgin. There is nothing we need be afraid to ask of her. There were Babylonian ex-votos to the goddess Ishtar carved in the rock two and a half thousand years before Christ by people petitioning for children and wealth. The Virgin Mary receives the same heartfelt pleas for fertility. Radiating joy in the fulfilment of the animal side of her human nature, the bountiful mother, or Alma Mater, is overflowing with tenderness and love. She appeals both to women who identify with her and to men who like to see in her their own mother, a female figure from whom desire and sexuality are conspicuously

MOTHER FIGURE

absent. Respectfully, the faithful kiss the gold-shod foot of Sansovino's sculpture of Madonna del Parto in San Agostino in Rome. In southern Italy, they present the Mother of God with a wedding gown. Humbly prostrated before her image, they speak in whispers, dazzled by her grace and bounty. The far rarer *virgo lactans* (the milk-giving Virgin) presents a very different idea of the body. This sensual image developed in the Coptic church of the ninth century out of the cult of Isis and its representations of a black goddess giving suck.

The Christians had lost no time in scraping the walls of the shelter in Bethlehem, said to be where Mary fed the infant Jesus. Since the first century AD, the white powder taken from these walls was soon connected with the idea of milk, and, like the holy relics, was at the core

Page 26: votive offering in the form
of a baby, of the type that used
to be given by grateful pregnant
women at Chartres or Loreto.
Page 27: the Holy Family of Our
Lady of Studzianna (seventeenth
century), presented to the Queen
of Poland by her father the
Habsburg Emperor Ferdinand II,
and pronounced 'miraculous'
some years later in 1671. This
rather curious portrayal of Mary

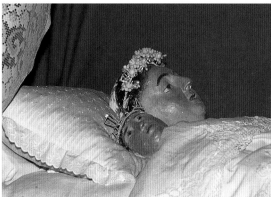

as nurturing mother has over
the years been liberally ornamented
with pearls.
Left: The chapel at Yaudet in
Brittany, on the site of a former
temple to Cybele. The Virgin Mary
is shown in childbed in a recess
in the eighteenth-century retable,
brought out only for processions.
The local people pray to her
for children, and say the rosary
to her each month.

of many stories of conversion. It was in this way that 'three drops of milk' were produced and arrived in Byzantium, before circulating throughout Europe. Charlemagne, the emperor of France, kept the holy milk in a medallion with a lock of the Virgin's hair, and took them with him into battle. When St Bernard prayed before a statue of the Virgin, he is supposed to have received a few drops of milk in his mouth.

In the Middle Ages, milk – the body transformed into food – was the relic that symbolized life. Fouquet's painting of the full breast of Agnès Sorel (the mistress of Charles VII of France) in his *Virgin with Child* effectively coincided with the banning of this

Left: Charlemagne used to wear round his neck this talisman containing three drops of the Virgin's milk and a lock of her hair. *Opposite*: in the fifteenth century, Charles VII of France asked Jean Fouquet to use his mistress Agnès Sorel as the model for a *Virgin with Child*. The picture caused a scandal.

extravagant cult, destined to reappear sporadically and in unexpected places. Our Lady of 'Crée-lait' is honoured in Nantes, Our Lady of 'Bon Lait' in Persac, near Poitiers. At Notre-Dame-du-Crann, a church in Brittany, a procession is held every summer around a huge mound of decorated butter. This virtual abstraction symbolizes fertility, in much the same way as the 'Great Mother' is sometimes represented in India as an ocean of milk that curdles, and in so doing creates the world.

In the seventeenth century, the Madonna's tears, another bodily secretion, took the place of the forbidden drops of holy milk. Tears, consisting of water, were just as much a source of life as milk. It seemed to the devout that the miraculous weeping madonnas were shedding tears for all their sins and their sorrows.

Virgo lactans – the
Virgin giving suck.
Left: the Virgin Mary's
milk, transformed into
a rosary of rubies, detail
from a painting of *The
Virgin of Belém* by the
Bolivian Melçhor Pérez de
Holguín, early eighteenth
century. According to
legend, Zeus put his son
Herakles to Hera's breast
while she was sleeping;
her flowing milk was
transformed into the Milky
Way. A similar story is
told of the Egyptian
goddess Hathor and the
Greek princess Io.
Top right: painting on
wood, Ethiopia,
eighteenth century.
Centre right: the Virgin
Galaktotrophusa ('milk-
giving'), Russia, sixteenth
century. The palm trees
are reminiscent of Isis.
Right below: a painting
of the Virgin on glass,
Peru, eighteenth century.

The black Virgins are the stars of the Marian cult. There are more than five hundred in Europe alone. Many made their appearance around the twelfth century, the age that produced the quest for the Holy Grail, the *Roman de la Rose* and the lyrical sermons of St Bernard, whose passion for the Virgin was such that he carried her image with him always. Some of the black Virgins are said to have been brought back by Crusaders, others arrived by boat, in mysterious circumstances.

The Catholic Church remains conspicuously silent on the matter of the Virgin's blackness. If you ask a priest, he will quickly reply that it is probably all due to the candlesmoke, or the age of the oak and walnut wood, or else caused by gunpowder. Among the most famous of these images are those of Our Lady of Kazan in Russia; of Czestochowa in Poland; Hal in Belgium; Einsiedeln in Switzerland; Mariazell in

BLACK VIRGINS

Austria; Chartres, Le Puy, Saint-Victor (Marseilles) and Rocamadour in France; and Guadalupe, Saragossa and Monserrat in Spain. Saragossa's is the oldest. According to the legend, James the Greater was in Spain in AD 40 (Santiago de Compostela, the great pilgrimage church, is dedicated to him); the Virgin Mary – who would still have been alive at this time – appeared to him and gave him the statue.

The black Virgin of Montserrat, 'La Moraneta' (the Little Black Lady), came from Judaea and was given to the Bishop of Barcelona in the late seventh century. When the Moors invaded, it was hidden away in the secret recesses of a magically fertile mountain, which had previously sheltered a temple dedicated to the Sumerian goddess Ishtar. It was rediscovered long after peace was restored by a 'poor shepherd', led to the spot by music and light quite as otherworldly as anything experienced at

5 ROCAMADOUR. - *Vue générale d'ensemble (côté est).* - LL

Fátima. Since then, a number of churches have been built on the mountainside, and a Benedictine monastery set up to serve her shrine. La Moraneta is in charge of fertility and sexuality. She presides over weddings and childbirth, and even revives stillborn babies. Her many miracles have attracted millions of pilgrims.

Rocamadour is on the route of the pilgrimage to Santiago de Compostela, and its black Virgin is reputed to be at least a thousand years old. There is a legend that it arrived by boat in the first century AD, brought from Palestine to Soulac by Zacchaeus and his wife Veronica. When Veronica died, Zacchaeus retreated to the top of a high rockface. Assuming the name Amadour ('lover of God'), he lived there as a hermit until his death around AD 70. His corpse was discovered intact in the twelfth century, near where the Virgin's statue stands today, and the site was called Rocamadour. Many eminent figures visited that rocky eminence, from St Louis of France to Henry II of England, climbing the 216 steps 'of expiation and redemption' leading up to the shrine to prostrate themselves before the slender silhouette. Seated on a throne, she and the Christ Child together embody the wisdom of God: the image is a *Sedes Sapientiae*, like the figures at Aurillac, Le Puy and Meymac, descended from Roman Cybele, originally from Asia Minor. The more royal visits there were to Rocamadour, the more symbolically 'charged' the site became. The more ancient the legend, the more deeply it was engraved on the collective consciousness. The more difficult the access, the greater the expiation. Who can say what makes it so sacred? Is it the mountain, the black Virgin, the Amadour's uncorrupted corpse or the magical

Previous page and opposite: the Virgin of Rocamadour, in south-west France, crudely carved, but with all the magic power of an African fetish. It is reputedly one thousand years old.
Top left: the rocky hillside of Rocamadour.

38

Top left: Our Lady of Einsiedeln (Switzerland). *Bottom left:* Our Lady of Saint-Victor (Marseilles). *Also on this page, centre left:* The black Virgins of the Auvergne – the *Sedes Sapientiae* of Orcival, Le Puy, Meymac, Aurillac, and several other places – all on the pilgrims' route to Compostela, bear a close resemblance to the Virgin of Rocamadour, and probably date from the twelfth century. *Opposite right*: La Moraneta (the Little Black Lady) of Monserrat in Spain, a miraculous image of the Virgin, arrived in Barcelona in the late seventh century, and was hidden for more than two hundred years in the mountain whose name it bears. It is also shown in the painting by the Benedictine monk Fray Juan de Rizi (*opposite*), seventeenth century.

Small miraculous images of the
Virgin are contained in vast
baroque retables. *Opposite*: Our
Lady of Mariazell in Austria.
Right and below: Our Lady of the
Pillar, in Saragossa in Spain,

surrounded by eighty gold stars
studded with precious stones, and
standing on a jasper pillar. This was
covered in silver to protect it from
the kisses of the faithful, who pray
to her in their millions each year.

properties of the earth that preserved it? Here the Virgin fulfils the function not only of black Isis the Egyptian on her boat, who is a mother and gives suck, but also of Ishtar and Gaia, two Mesopotamian goddesses identified with mother earth, the mountains, rocks, caverns and damp disturbing clefts which hold the secret of life.

In the twelfth century a young scholar from Chartres visited the Auvergne and was shocked to see the tributes paid to 'these bits of wood half-covered with gold, of barbaric luxury'. At a time when magnificent and imposing cathedrals were being built all over Europe, these rough-hewn tree trunks must have had a raw power more reminiscent of symbolic fetishes from some primeval age. Those of more traditional appearance, at Chartres and Saragossa for example, resemble the handmaiden of the Lord in Solomon's Song of Songs: 'I am black but comely'. There are members of the clergy who would not be uncomfortable with that view. But these mythic beings may also be identified with mysterious and evil creatures associated with the invisible forces of magic, with the demon Lilith and with Kali, the Indian goddess who is both creator and destroyer. These exotic associations would expand the devout imagination, enabling Christians to assimilate outside elements into their faith.

There is undoubtedly an alternative power at work here, that attracts many different human beings. The proof is the pilgrimage to Chartres Cathedral during the month of May of hundreds of Tamils, who have nowhere to worship their goddess Kali. They wear bright clothes, prostrate themselves on the ground or hang votive scarves on Gothic pillars; they direct their prayers to the small statue of the Virgin and Child that has been an object of veneration for centuries of Catholic kings, and which flickers in the candlelight under the quizzical gaze of priests confronting the breadth of the phenomenon.

Left: the black Virgin of Hal in Belgium, thirteenth century. She is dressed in eighteenth-century lace and blue velvet. Her crown, which dates from 1874, was paid for by the donations of the faithful. As she has on several occasions 'defended' the town, some believe her dark colour was caused by gunpowder from the cannon balls still preserved in the church. Two other precious relics are pieces of the veil of the 'real' Virgin. The first (*opposite*) is kept in a silver-gilt 'mystic rose'; the other (*above*) in a reliquary in the form of a medallion. The treasury in the crypt of the basilica displays gifts presented to the black Virgin by Henry VIII of England and Louis XII of France.

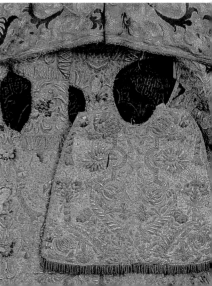

Preceding double-page, opposite and left: Notre-Dame du Pilier, Chartres, sixteenth century. The black Virgin carved in pear wood is honoured today in Chartres Cathedral, having gradually supplanted Notre-Dame sous Terre, a twelfth-century *Sedes Sapientiae*. She is surrounded by votive offerings of hearts, one (*page 44, top right*) given in 1791 by Mme Elisabeth, sister of Louis XVI. The Virgins of Chartres possessed several fine robes. *Opposite and left*: robe of Lucca velvet trimmed with ermine, fifteenth century, and brocade robe, seventeenth and eighteenth centuries.

The believer communicates with the Virgin in two ways, through supplication and thanksgiving, both acts accompanied by votive offerings, perhaps candles, alms or 'anatomical' images indicating the site of an illness. Requests may also be written in a spiral-bound notebook at the Virgin's feet. But the ex-voto may take an even more bizarre form. When Pope John Paul II escaped an assassination attempt in 1981, it is said he had the bullet that spared his life covered in gold and sent to Our Lady of Fátima because the attack occurred on the anniversary of her apparition. And in the past, when the aristocratic ladies of France and Italy gave birth to a male heir, they would give their baby's weight in gold to the Virgin who had answered their prayers. And at the French Revolution a young woman repenting of her debaucheries gave her evening gown and cape of peacock

VOTIVE OFFERINGS

feathers to the Virgin of Notre-Dame-du-Roncier at Josselin in Brittany. Yet the most moving offerings by far are the pictures of boats that have survived storms, and the thousands of hearts made of gold or silver, paste or cardboard with which the faithful have expressed their uncomplicated devotion since the seventeenth century.

The churches and chapels of present-day Europe are being emptied of these wonderful testaments of faith. On the one hand, civil servants remove anything of value to a museum, while, on the other, the clergy discourages further excesses. At Chartres, the hearts are being cleared away 'for reasons of space'. Thieves take care of whatever is left of all these tangible proofs of naive and popular faith, now felt to be too pagan.

Opposite centre: candles in multicoloured plastic pots have tended to replace traditional candles. *Above*: the green candles of the black Virgin of Saint-Victor in Marseilles, who will accept no other colour. The Virgin is supposed to have arrived in Marseilles from Egypt by boat, a magical event commemorated by a biscuit (*below*) sold in the *pâtisserie* opposite the church.

50

Simeon made this prediction to Mary in the Gospels, : 'Behold, for this child is set... for a sign which sh[...] be spoken against; Yea, a sword sh[...] pierce through thy own soul also that [...] thoughts of many hearts shall be reveale[...] The image of the sword was to gain w[...] currency, most frequently in represen[...] tions of the Sacred Heart of Jes[...] In the twelfth century, the Flem[...] mystic Lutgard of Aywières saw [...] apparition of Christ. 'What [...] you want of me?' she ask[...] him. 'Your heart,' came [...] reply. 'Give me yours [...] exchange,' she respond[...] In the seventee[...] century, Ch[...] showed [...] heart

St Marguerite-
Marie Alacoque as she
was in ecstasy, saying, 'This is the
[he]art that so loved men.' First the
[Do]minicans and then the Jesuits adopted
[the] heart as the symbol of the Christian
[fait]h. In the seventeenth century, the
[sor]rows of the Virgin were set at seven.
[An]d when Pius XI established the Feast of
[the] Sacred Heart in 1856, the heart of the
[Vir]gin with its crown of roses, trans-
[fix]ed by a sword, was beside the heart
[of] Christ bleeding under its crown
[of] thorns. The most popular
[he]art ex-voto, usually made of
[gol]d, silver or enamel, is a
[littl]e container inside
[wh]ich the supplicant
[sli]des a vow on
[a ti]ny slip of
[pap]er.

52

El día 14 de Junio del año de 1746, en el Pueblo de Santiago Matallan, estando bajando
mazorcas de una troje, Joseph Antonio de los Angeles cayó en el suelo, e invo-
cando el nombre de Maria Santissima de la Soledad, se lebantó, illesso, y sano

Right: the patron saint of coral fishers, Our Lady of Constantinople at Torre del Greco in Italy, on the Bay of Naples. In Provence (*opposite above*) and Mexico (*opposite below*) votive offerings in the form of paintings tell the stories of the many occasions on which the Virgin rescued a sailor or peasant from impending disaster.

Opposite: rarer now are the anatomical ex-votos, which here resemble works of modern art. There are arms, legs, heads, even stomachs, hearts and bladders. These days the faithful are more likely to use colour photos or scraps of garments that have touched the part of the body they want to protect or heal.
Left: in areas with a strong agricultural tradition, the Virgin will sometimes be asked to watch over someone's pig or cow.
Below: votive rags beside the holy spring of the Virgin's House near Ephesus in Turkey.

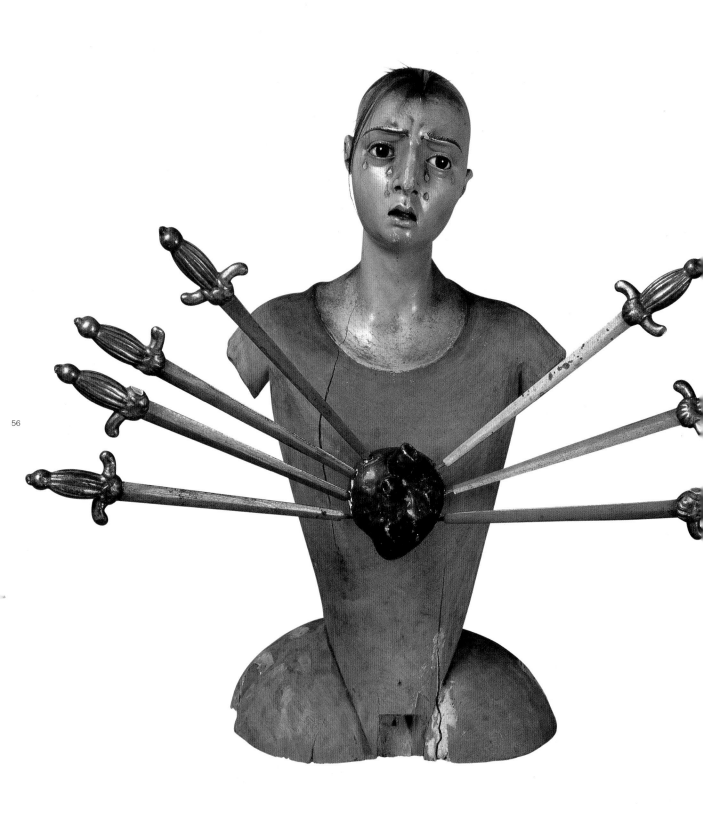

56

All the ancient Mediterranean civilizations from Asia Minor to Egypt were initiated into the violent and lugubrious mourning rituals of the cults of ancient goddesses like Inanna, Ishtar, Isis and Cybele. The three last were among many who grieved for the death of a son (sometimes a brother) as well as lover, uttering cries of despair, tearing their hair and rending their flesh with their nails until the youth was restored to life, symbolizing the coming of spring. In the twelfth century, St Bernard of Clairvaux – confidant of popes, campaigner for the Second Crusade and archetypal figure of Christianity – devoted numerous poems and sermons to the sufferings of the Virgin Mary. The Mater Dolorosa did not however fully emerge until the Middle Ages, when it appeared simultaneously in France, Italy, England and Spain. In the Gospels, Simeon predicted to Mary that 'a sword shall pierce through thy own soul also'.

SEVEN SORROWS

By the seventeenth century, the Church had fixed the number of her sorrows at seven: Simeon's prophecy, the flight to Egypt at the time of the massacre of the Innocents, the disappearance of Jesus in the Temple at the age of twelve, the Calvary, the Crucifixion, the Deposition from the Cross and the Entombment.

The Franciscans had a particular fondness for pictures of the Mater Dolorosa and the Pietà – no doubt because St Francis in ecstasy received the stigmata on his hands (as in the twentieth century did the Italian Padre Pio, beatified by John Paul II in 1999). Since the sixteenth century, Christians have thrilled to the famous *Stabat Mater,* attributed to Jacopone da Todi, and its musical settings by Josquin des Prez, Palestrina, Haydn, Rossini and Pergolesi. The *Stabat Mater* describes Christ's Passion through the eyes of his Mother: 'Stabat mater dolorosa....' Jacopone da Todi wrote it after a life of dissolution, of which he repented on his wife's death. Pergolesi died in a monastery at Pozzuoli at the age of twenty-six shortly after completing his grandiose and sensual score. 'Oh how sad and sore distressed was that mother, highly blest…. Can the human heart refrain from partaking in her pain.' It was the terrible Black Death, the great epidemic of the plague, which spread from Asia to Europe in the fourteenth century, that turned what might have been a temporary phenomenon into a permanent feature of the Marian cult. As a mother, the Virgin mourns not only for her son but for all the faithful who are her children.

Today, in Italy, Sicily, Mexico, Latin America and above all in Seville in Spain, the ceremonies of Holy Week leading up to Easter, and the death and resurrection of Jesus, demonstrate the activities of the cult at their most extreme. Between Palm Sunday and Easter Day, fifty statues of Jesus and Mary emerge from the churches of Seville, to be carried one behind the other in an extraordinary procession all around the town.

The young women of Seville wear the devoutly respectable black lace mantilla, even if, in contrast, their skirts are often very short and their lipstick very bright. On heavy floats, borne by sweating and half-naked men, the lifesize statues, surrounded by hundreds of candles, tower above carpets of carnations and roses whose perfumes mingle with those of the

Page 56: unusually, the Virgin of the Seven Sorrows is shown here undressed, without her formal robes; southern Italy, eighteenth century.
Opposite: the Virgin of the Sorrows dressed in her robes for the Holy Thursday procession; Antigua, Guatemala. *Left*: wooden figurine by Arroyo Hondo Santero; New Mexico, 1830–40.

flowering orange trees along the route. Under embroidered canopies are displayed weeping Pietàs, the son's body draped over the mother's knees, or solitary images of the Mater Dolorosa, dressed for the occasion in a robe with a train and crowned with a diadem. Handkerchief in hand, they extend their arms and incline their head to the faithful, lace veil partly concealing their features, their carved faces glittering with crystal tears. Half-queen, half-goddess, Maria Santissima de las Angustias vies with her counterparts – de la Merced, de las Lágrimas, de los Dolores, de las Penas – for the emotion of the crowd. The huge semi-human dolls sometimes bear the signature of famous sculptors such as Juan de Mesa or Juan Martínez Montañés, while others are mawkish and sentimental. The most highly venerated are called after their districts of Seville – La Esperanza de la Macarena, and Nuestra Señora de Triana – and process on Good Friday, the day of the Crucifixion, when the population crowds the streets. Alternating with them are El Silencio and El Gran Poder – figures of Christ in his Passion. Each of these images is presented by its own 'confraternity', a group of the faithful dedicated to Mary, Jesus or the saints, who perform charitable works in the secular world. The confraternities of Seville are power-ful organizations. That of El Silencio for example, founded in the fourteenth century, or of La Macarena, which dates from the sixteenth century, have a member-ship of two and a half thousand, while that of La Triana has between nineteen hundred and two thousand members, a large proportion of whom are homosexuals, gypsies and sailors, on whom this Virgin confers special protection.

There is much tension and rivalry between the different groups, who organize ever more ostentatious displays and secret rituals. These performances are theatrical as much as they are religious, and the people of Seville are attuned to nuances outsiders

Page 60: the lifesize statue of
La Esperanza de Macarena,
Seville, carried on a float in the
nocturnal Good Friday procession.
Page 61: La Macarena (detail).
The necklace that she is wearing
is made of emeralds.
Right: La Macarena (detail).
Her sleeves are made of eighteenth-

century lace, and she holds a
rosary of precious stones.
Above: La Macarena seen from
the back, wearing a robe with
train, dating from around 1900,
paid for by charity bullfights.
Opposite: the same dress pictured
on an embroidered postcard.

could not begin to appreciate. Thus, a poorly decorated float carried at too great a speed is as disastrous for the confraternity as a bankruptcy or a failed deal.

Matadors, whose first corridas take place on Easter Sunday, have a particular connection with the Madonna. Each matador has his personal Virgin. The two are almost like a married couple, translated to the mythic scale. If the matador emerges unscathed from a particularly hazardous fight, he offers his protective Virgin his 'suit of lights' to attach to the train of her dress. If his life is in danger following a corrida, he asks for the Virgin's cape to be placed over his hospital bed.

Fed on these myths and legends, the crowd in this culture of machismo shouts to the

Virgin as if she were a beautiful woman passing by. The people seem to be held in a collective state of trance, the mood becoming more tragic as night falls. From packed balconies, carnations and rose petals rain down. In the eyes of some, these 'magic' rituals have a cathartic power. They release repressed and pent-up anxieties, offer consolation and hope. For others, such trashy and grandiose displays have little to do with the true faith, and only encourage Christians to be masochists and women to be passive. The cult of tears, in all its sensational representations, was of course a substitute for the cult of the Virgin's milk, banned by the Church in the fifteenth century. In Italy and Chile, more than fifty Madonnas are said to have cried real tears since 1990; one plaster statue in Syracuse in Sicily even cried tears of blood for four whole days. Since 1953, there have been several attempts to provide scientific analyses and justifications for mysteries that continued to defy explanation. But if the tears of the Virgin have such power to stimulate the imagination, it is because they incarnate both human misery and redemption. Like water, they represent a rebirth: life itself, springtime, flows from those emblematic eyes.

Page 64: Maria Santissima de la Guadalupe, Chapel of the Rosary, Seville, wearing a 1930s headdress.
Page 65: Nuestra Señora de las Angustias of Seville with her lace veil – the same in black is worn by women of Seville at religious festivals. Both images express their grief with crystal tears.
Opposite: Rosa Mistica from San Damiano in Italy – a miraculous plaster statue that began to cry tears of blood in 1982.
Top left: Virgen Dolorosa, Peru.
Bottom left: Spanish nineteenth-century painting on glass.
Bottom right: the Virgin from Seville's district of Triana in her 1930s costume as patron saint of sailors.

QUEEN OF HEAVEN

It was in 1954 that the Church officially conferred on Mary the title of Queen of Heaven, but even in the tenth century the Pope chanted the *Regina Coeli*, and the twelfth-century Cistercians invented the famous *Salve Regina*.
Left: baroque chapel in the Azores.
Opposite: crown by the Parisian jewelers Boucheron (*top left*); Spanish Virgin with Child (*top right*); Brazilian Virgin with dove (*bottom left*); Our Lady of Grace, Knock, Ireland (*bottom right*); three medieval French Virgins (*centre*).

The procession is the most modest form of pilgrimage, when the faithful carry the statue of their patron saint around their church, village or island as part of the local festival. Like the statue, they are dressed in their best as they parade, bearing the image aloft so the saint can bless the places where they lead their everyday lives. Such practices are very common in Brittany. Every six years, for the period of a week, the 'Grande Troménie' of Locronan leads its pilgrims through twelve kilometres of countryside, along an ancient route marked with magic stones of Celtic origin that takes in miraculous springs and Druidic forests. The ceremony coincides with the festival of Lug, Celtic spirit of fertility and the harvest.

In Spain, the pilgrimage of Our Lady of El Rocío (of 'the dew'), held every seven years at Pentecost, attracts more than a million and a half pilgrims. The story relates

PROCESSIONS

once again how during the fifteenth century a statue with beautiful and enigmatic features was discovered under a bush on the marshes of Almonte, near Cadiz, by a lost boar hunter, brought to the spot by a bright lily and strange music. The tale goes on to tell how he took the statue home and fell asleep, only to discover when he awoke that it had returned to the marshes (where the pilgrimage is still held today), and was covered in dew.

In these two magnificent landscapes, the processions celebrate the Creator's works. Open to the skies, they show how nature is part of the ritual, encouraging the believer to reconcile his perception of the world with his faith, and experience the transcendental in the wonders of the visible world.

BRETAGNE (Finistère)

Locronan. — Pardon de la Troménie. — Après un parcours, la Procession fait le tour de la Place et de l'Eglise.

Page 71 and pages 76–79: procession of Our Lady of El Rocío, not far from Cadiz. *Page 70 and right*: the procession at Locronan, Brittany. Both are spectacular affairs, passing through beautiful countryside. At Locronan, several images of the Virgin accompany St Ronan on the 'Grande Troménie', which takes a week to follow a twelve-kilometre route through the fields. *Opposite*: Feast of the Assumption, near Cracow, Poland. The women hold the ends of ribbons attached to the Virgin.

Between Easter and the Feast of the Assumption on 15 August, the most venerated statues emerge from all the churches and even the tiniest chapels to celebrate their feast days. Dressed in their best, the Virgins are borne aloft by the men. The other villagers follow in procession, with banners and crosses, throwing coloured powder or bright flower petals underfoot. The procession usually ends in a lively party, with sausages, lanterns and accordions. *Above and below right*: processions in Bolivia and in Brittany. *Opposite*: procession in Provence (*top left*); Hierro in the Canary Islands (*bottom left*); procession in Guatemala (*right*).

THE HOLY HOU

SES OF LORETO

Preceding double-page and right: in Italy, since the fourteenth century, countless different images have been produced of Our Lady of Loreto and the Santa Casa, the Virgin's Holy House, venerated by fifty popes. Originally the Virgin was white and neoclassical in style, but then took the form of a black Virgin, always wearing a tubular dress, often of precious materials (*right*).

Opposite, bottom right: eighteenth-century lampas (similar to brocades) ornamented with pearls, precious stones and embroidered satin, with a ribbon certifying the garment has been worn by the 'true' statue.

Opposite, top left: the Santa Casa – the house that flew from Nazareth – has also appeared in many different forms at different periods, and also in the interpretations of individual artists.

82

According to legend, in 1291, when the Saracens reached Nazareth, the angels decided to move the Virgin Mary's house to a safe place. They took it first to Dalmatia, but judged the faithful to be insufficiently devout, and transported it instead to Loreto, south of Ancona in Italy. The move was approved by the Virgin in a fourteenth-century apparition. Various miracles ensued. Sixteen stout knights were even sent to verify the dimensions of the house's foundations in Palestine.

Even before this, in 1061 at Walsingham in England the Virgin was said to have appeared to a holy woman, and asked her to build a house like the Holy House in Nazareth. Until this was demolished by Protestants in 1538, it was a highly revered shrine, for which England was known as 'Our Lady's Dowry'. The Santa Casa of Loreto took its place. As with the Veil at Chartres, the Santa Casa is regarded as more holy than the statue of the Virgin itself. Because it has been touched by Mary herself, it has the status of a relic. Rather in the manner of a Russian doll, it was enclosed within a white marble reliquary by Bramante, which in turn was installed inside a basilica surrounded by walls – from which the monks would collect 'miracle' dust for sale. The faithful who penetrate these narrow confines receive protection or an answer to their prayers. By virtue of its miraculous journey through the air, the Santa Casa also has the power to watch over pilots. Napoleon saw Loreto as a 'temple of superstition' – and took advantage of that judgment to remove a number of works of art to the Louvre.

In the sixteenth century, on his arrival in Mexico, Hernando Cortés the Spanish Catholic conquistador was confronted with a native Indian population who worshipped many different gods and performed human sacrifice. The peoples of the Andes also paid homage to an earth-mother goddess called the Pachamama or Santa Tierra, who assumed the form of a mountain. For the Indians, every living creature and every thing – flower, moon, rain, thunder, hail – was inhabited by divine forces or *huacas*, similar to the fairies of Celtic lands, whom it was necessary to placate. For a long time, the conquistadores set about the systematic destruction of the Aztec culture, under the pretext that the Indians had no souls. The two civilizations were poles apart, whether in their definitions of property, death, equality or time, or their understanding of collective action or the role of women – who, like the men, found

SYNCRETISM

themselves treated by the Spaniards as slaves or sex objects. It was against this violent and dramatic background that the Virgin of Guadalupe appeared, ten years after the conquest of Mexico. Nine million Indians were converted in six years. Today she is a symbol of national identity for Latin Americans all over the world.

In 1531, a young Indian peasant called Juan Diego was on a hill called Tepeyac, when he heard the strains of wonderful music. A beautiful 'Lady' appeared to him with a request that he ask Bishop Zumárraga of Mexico to build a chapel there. The bishop demanded a sign, and the Lady then asked Juan Diego to gather some flowers to present to him. By this time winter had set in, but Juan Diego found some sweet-smelling roses, gathered them into his rough agave cape and returned to Zumárraga. When he opened the cape to let the roses fall to the ground, the bishop was stupefied

NON FECIT TALITER OMNI NATIONI

to discover the image of the Lady imprinted on the garment. On the spot where the apparition took place, there was previously a shrine dedicated to the pre-Columbian goddess Coatlicue, mother of the sun and moon. The coincidence was not lost on the Indians, and they interpreted all the details of the woman's costume with reference to ancient Aztec tradition. When Juan Diego asked her name, she is supposed to have replied 'Coatlocpia'. This the Spanish transliterated as 'Guadalupe', the name of the famous image of the Virgin, much venerated by Cortés, which had been presented by Pope Gregory I to Seville in the sixth century, then hidden from the Moors to be rediscovered near the river of Guadalupe in the fourteenth century.

The Indians also equated Mary with Omecihuatl, the mother of their creator. The fact that the apparition had dark features was explained, in the Spaniards' eyes, by her Moorish or Byzantine origins; for the Indians by her membership of their own ethnic group. They even concluded that she was pregnant, because she wore a belt with a pompom and a flower that they associated with fertility. For them, the blue of her veil was the colour of the goddess Omecihuatl, while her red dress recalled Coatlicue's son, god of war and of the sun, Huitzilopochtli, 'he who gives and preserves life by drinking blood'. The flowers around her were like those associated with the god Quetzalcoatl. So the Indian community discovered in the Virgin Mary an extension of their own beliefs. She was a source of hope, a recourse in time of need. As 'La Guadalupe', she was honoured in a transformed but just acceptable version of Spanish Catholic ritual. Today the Virgin of Guadalupe has a site on the Internet, where there is a colour portrait and an electronic rendition of *Ave Maria*.

This process of assimilation was repeated in southern Mexico, Bolivia, Brazil, Peru and all over South America. The famous statue of Our Lady of Soledad of Oaxaca is said to have arrived mysteriously in a chest carried on muleback over the mountains. Arrayed in gold-embroidered velvet strewn with pearls, she became the patron saint of sailors, because the sound of waves was always heard near her and her skirts smelled of iodine and salt. The Yucatán Indians were yet others who identified the Virgin Mary with the mother-goddess Coatlicue. The town of Mérida enjoyed the protection of Our Lady of the Incarnation, Izamal that of Our Lady of the Immaculate Conception. The Franciscans, who were in the Yucatán in large numbers, celebrated mass in pagan temples while they waited for churches to be built, a series of miracles having accelerated the pace of evangelization.

In Cuzco (the capital of the ancient Inca empire) and the rest of Peru, in Bolivia and throughout the Andes, the Virgin and Child superseded the Pachamama as a fertility symbol, although to this day the miners of the mountain that she inhabits at Potosí in southern Bolivia make offerings to their earth-mother goddess of maize, llama foetuses, beans and wine, in return for help in finding a good vein of silver.

In Brazil, the gods had already experienced one change of identity when they arrived from Africa with the slave trade, before they acquired Catholic names and functions. The Virgin of the Immaculate Conception was associated with Yemanja, fertility symbol and Queen of the Sea. Which is why she has always been portrayed more as a sensual and opulent Venus than a modest young woman from Nazareth.

Page 85: the Virgin of Guadalupe. On her right is an important figure wearing ermine, who symbolizes Europe, on her left a 'savage' with a feather skirt, who represents America; anonymous, Mexico, eighteenth century. *Opposite and top right*: cartouches telling the story of the apparition of the Virgin (details of the picture on the preceding page).

Throughout America, from Mexico to New York, the Virgin of Guadalupe inspires passionate devotion. Her image is found everywhere, cropping up on the most unlikely objects (*left*).

Opposite: a tattoo of the Virgin of Guadalupe with the inscription 'The Queen of My Life'; photograph by Louis Carlos Bernal (1941–93), *The Mother of My Life*.

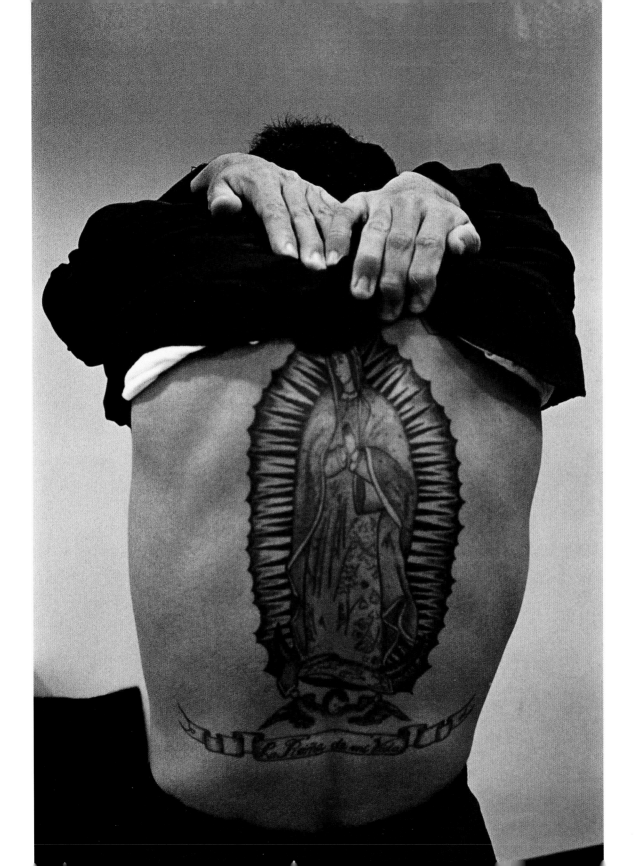

Page 90: the Virgin of the Rosary,
wearing a head-dress of a Coya
(or queen) of the Andes, school of
Cuzco, Peru, eighteenth century.
Page 91 (detail) and below: the
Virgin of Pomata by José de Arce,
Peru, seventeenth century.
Top and bottom left: in Bolivia,
the Virgin is often accompanied by
angels, sometimes dressed as Spanish
soldiers, in Roman costumes or
even women's clothes. They have
replaced the Inca gods of the wind,
the harvest, lightning and the clouds,
and play a role similar to that
of fairies in the lore of Celtic
civilizations; anonymous, Bolivia,
seventeenth century.
Right: the Virgin as Pachamama,
in her earthly incarnation as the
silver-mining mountain of Potosí.
Double page overleaf: detail of the
hem of the Virgin of Bélem's robe,
with its images of the sun and moon,
objects of worship for the Incas;
Melchor Pérez de Holguín, Bolivia,
early eighteenth century.

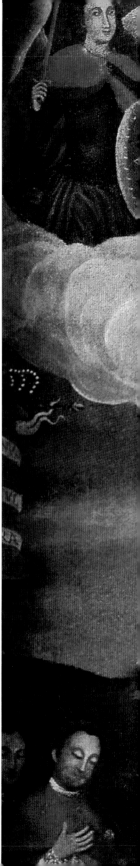

When Mariolatry was at its height, in the twelfth and nineteenth centuries, for example, wayside shrines to the local Virgin were set up on street corners and in the hollows of trees. Only to remain there forgotten until destroyed or decapitated by the actions of the French Revolution or some secular or Communist state.

When a stranger visits an important and distant Marian shrine, he takes home with him all sorts of devotional objects, including the obligatory reproductions of the local Virgin. In the past, when a Breton sailor disembarked in Marseilles after a long voyage, he would buy a fragile *santibelli* made of earthenware thinly coated with gold. It enjoyed pride of place on the mantelshelf, beside the Jersey china dogs and the Chinese Buddhas from Hong Kong. The fishermen who plied

SHRINES

their trade off Newfoundland used to take a chapel in miniature on board ship.

In the eighteenth century, Father Dionisi devoted a treatise to the correct manner of honouring the Virgin Mary. As still happens in Mexico today, you were advised to set up a small altar and 'decorate' it 'artistically grouping candelabras and urns around it'. The flowers to be used were lily-of-the-valley, wallflowers and above all the hawthorn, which, like the lily, is traditionally dedicated to Mary.

In our own times such practices are much less common, but the statues remain, cropping up in the most unexpected places. Often poetically if sometimes incongruously decorated, they offer a window on to the past. Nobody knows when they were put there or by whom, as the race memory rarely goes back more than three generations. Timeless, old-fashioned, pure kitsch, they are echoes of a lost civilization.

Page 96: a 'Marseilles Virgin' on a Breton dresser.
Page 97: in Ireland, the Virgin watches over the workers in a tweed factory.
Right: pictures of the beloved Virgin of Guadalupe in a peasant house in Mexico.
Bottom left: painting of the Virgin and Child in an elegant drawing room in the Canary Islands.
Bottom right: Mexican villagers on a visit to the capital have their photographs taken with the Virgin of Guadalupe.

98

A statuette of the Virgin of Guadalupe in the home of Mexican peasants (*top left*). A tiny chapel in the mountains of Morvan in France, built over a magic spring, near an ancient tree (*top right*); and a shrine in a grotto in Andalusia (*left*), which receives hundreds of offerings and ex-votos every year.

Preceding double page: the market at Ajaccio, Corsica.
Right: statues of the Virgin: a Mexican street (*top left*); Seville (*bottom left*); a street in Lecce, southern Italy (*bottom right*).
Below: a Swiss devotional object representing the black Virgin of Einsiedeln, intended to be displayed above a bed.

Opposite: all over France, you still come across statues of the Virgin Mary in niches in the wall and above doorways – they were thought to protect the house: the Meuse, north-eastern France (*left*), and Finistère in Brittany (*right*).

103

In 1854, Pope Pius IX pronounced the dogma of the Immaculate Conception, which states that Mary, who brought Jesus into the world without benefit of human intervention, was herself conceived without 'stain of original sin'. One hundred years later, the Church proclaimed the dogma of the Assumption, according to which the Virgin Mary died and ascended into heaven with her flesh uncorrupted. Between these two definitions of dogma, visions of the Virgin proliferated, and vast and frequently hideous basilicas were built in her name: at Pontmain (1871) in France, Knock (1879) in Ireland, Castelpetroso (1888) in southern Italy, Fátima (1917) in Portugal, among others. The 'Lady' always appeared to poor people, innocents – shepherds as often as not – in isolated country places. The stories all follow a familiar pattern, and involve bushes, grottoes, music and mysterious light. The figure is

MODERN TIMES

dressed in white, and sometimes has a belt or a rosary, or a snake underfoot. She is alone, young and beautiful, her hands joined in prayer and eyes downcast.

Probably the most famous vision is Our Lady of Lourdes, who appeared to Bernadette Soubirous just four years after the pronouncement of the dogma of the Immaculate Conception. Some five million pilgrims visit her shrine each year, many of them invalids. One hundred and fifty hotels accommodate them, and five hundred shops satisfy their need for devotional objects. They drink water from the spring discovered by Bernadette, and bathe in it, and parade day and night with flaming torches following a precise ritual. Mass pilgrimages have been coming to Lourdes from Ireland since 1883, and there is even a separate counter for Lourdes at Dublin airport.

Page 104: an old statue of the Virgin Mary 'repainted' by artist Lili Fontazzi.

Page 105: chromo-lithograph of the 1870 apparition of Our Lady of Knock – the tiny village of Knock, in Ireland, was besieged by pilgrims, and finally decided to build an international airport in 1986.

Top left: statue of the Virgin, a copy of Our Lady of Lourdes, by the roadside in the Jura.

Bottom right: a Virgin that lights up when you put a coin in the slot, from a chapel in Auray, Brittany. The luminous statues are all for the bedside table, as such devotional objects are found worldwide even as far afield as Indonesia (bottom left).

Opposite: at Ballinspittle, near Cork in Ireland, the faithful wait in the rain for the Virgin to give them a sign; another identical copy of Our Lady of Lourdes, she is said to move.

Officiel: un miraculé de plus à Lourdes

En 1987, un sclérosé repart guéri. Onze ans d'enquête de l'Église pour viser le miracle

The Irish have also created replica grottoes of their own for the less well-off, like the miraculous grotto of Inchicore at Stillogan, which resembles a cave you might find in the Jura in the French heartlands or the shrine in the chapel at Auray in Brittany.

Our Lady of Lourdes is not with child like the Virgin of Guadalupe, she does not have the tenderness of Our Lady of Kazan, or the grief of La Macarena. She is an abstraction, the supernatural incarnation of a disembodied female principle. Because her origins are 'without stain', there is no hint of human passion in her. An apparition bathed in unearthly white light, she is always portrayed with a bland realism. All she exists for is to intercede with God on our behalf.

The artists of the modern world have tended to resist this tired yet all-pervasive cliché. In 1865, Julia Margaret Cameron photographed a *Beata*, and Cecil Beaton used Diana Manners as his model for a *Madonna* in 1928. In 1958 Salvador Dalí painted his wife Gala as a baroque Guadalupe. In 1991, Pierre et Gilles photographed the singer Lio as La Macarena in *Coeur blessé* and Nina Hagen as Mary in *La Sainte Famille*. Just as the king of France had his mistress painted as the Virgin, so the artists of today pose famous people as the Virgin, the eternal female archetype. Artist Cindy Sherman chose to photograph herself as the Virgin, and the singer Madonna borrowed her name and image as a personal trademark. In a more abstract vein, in 1956 the artist Catharina Fritsch piled up a number of statuettes of Our Lady of Lourdes. In 1998, adopting a more naive approach, Lili Fontazzi repainted old statues of Mary with fantastic decorations. Artist Bettina Rheims remains an isolated example with her 'blasphemous' images. As for haute couture and magazines like *Elle*, *Vogue* and *Harper's Bazaar*, they continue to treat the Virgin Mary as a sort of 'glamour' object, part princess and part fairy, the stuff of dreams.

Opposite above: the Virgin of Fátima emerging from a sheaf of lilies and white carnations as she looks down on the flaming torches of a nocturnal procession in Portugal. It is like a scene from Woodstock music festival. *Opposite below*: a 3-D image of Our Lady of Fátima on a holographic postcard (*left*); a fan and postcard (*centre*) with pictures of Francisco, Jacinta and Lucia, the 'three poor peasant children', who witnessed her apparition (*right*).

108

Jacinta Francisco Lúcia

Art and fashion have turned away from the ubiquitous insipid image of Our Lady of Lourdes. *Opposite*: Cindy Sherman posing as the Virgin Mary, 1989 (*left*); *The Virgin of Guadalupe* by Salvador Dalí, 1959 (*top right*); *Beata* by Julia Margaret Cameron, 1865 (*below right*). *Below*: J.-F. Schyder, *Madonna and Child*, Basle, 1976–82.

Right: all the fashion magazines and top couturiers have at some point been inspired by the Virgin Mary. Here, her image appears on a top by Dolce & Gabbana (1998).

ACKNOWLEDGMENTS

This book is based on material drawn from the author's personal collections. It would not exist were it not for her friends: M. Boisseuil, C. De Bresson, C. Cairns, J. Cardon, E. Ciborowski, A. Clavier, V. Darré, M. Ducaté, A. Emery, P. Gabrielse, D. Gaumont, F. Gilles, C. Gollut, N. Greenwood, M. Herold, M. Hogg, M. Isorio-Farinha, Y. Marie, M. Marquez, F. Passera, P. Renaud, J.L. Robequin, B. Saalburg, R. de Saint-Amand, M. Soszinsca, I. Terestchenko, B. Turle, A. Vassiliev, B. Wirth.

PHOTOGRAPHIC CREDITS

(*a* = above, *b* = below, *c* = centre, *l* = left, *r* = right)

Institute of Ethiopian Studies, Addis Ababa: 33 *a*
Photo AKG, London: 17 (Tretjakov Gallery, Moscow), 31 (Koninklijk Museum voor Schone Kunsten, Antwerp), 40 (Wallfahrtskirche, Mariazell, Austria/photo Erich Lessing), 90 (Monasterio de Santa Catalina, Cuzco, Peru/photo Veintimilla), 94–95 (Museo de la Casa de la Moneda/photo Veintimilla)
Ankara Museum: 13 *a*   **Photo Archives Photographiques, Paris**: 26, 67 *bc*   **Photo Artes de Mexico**: 52 *bl & br*, 85–87
Courtesy the author: 2, 18, 23 *a & b*, 32, 36, 38 *v & ix*, 43 *l*, 44 *bl*, 52 *a*, 53, 62, 63 *l*, 65, 67 *bl & br*, 69 *ac & bl*, 70, 75 *al & bl*, 78–79, 88 *al*, 92 *a & b*, 96, 97, 98 *bl*, 103 *r*, 104, 106 *c & br*, 109 *br & bcr*   **Museum für Gegenwarkstkunst, Basel**. Photo Martin Bühler, Basel: 111 *l*   **Photo Roland Beaufre**: 1, 12, 42, 43 *r*, 44 *al & ar & br*, 45–49, 50 *ac & ar & c & bc*, 51 *al & ac & bl*, 88 *bc*, 102 *ar & br*, 106 *ac & cl & bc*, 112   **Loaned by Lisa and Katrina Bernal**: 89   **Photo M. Blanschong**: 28, 29
Photo Boyadjian: 50 *al & bl & br*; 51 *c & br*, 56, 67 *bl*   **National Museum of Photography, Film and Television, Bradford**/photo Science & Society Picture Library, London: 110 *br*   **Photo Janet Brooke**: 55 *r*   **Courtesy Boucheron, Paris**: 69 *al*   **Photo R. Delon/Castelet**: 35, 37   **Photo Eric Cattin**: 73, 74 *b*
With permission of Joan Carroll Cruz/private collection: 58
© **Salvador Dalí** – Foundation Gala – Salvador Dalí/DACS 2000/private collection: 110 *ar*   **Photo Editions Debaisieux**: 38 *ii, iii, vi, vii*
© **FISA, Barcelona**: 67 *ar*, 109 *bl*   Collection Peter Gabrielse: 55 *l*

Photo D. Gaumont: 99 *ar*   **Photo G. Gayral**: 38 *viii*   **From La Historia della Chiesa di Santa Maria de Loreto, with permission of Floriano Grimaldi**: 82–83   **From Iconografia della Virgine de Loreto, with permission of Floriano Grimaldi**: 80–81   **Photo © Niall McInerney**: 111 *r*   **Photo © Bruno Barbey/Magnum**: 72   **Photo Eric Morin**: 100–101   **New Orleans Museum of Art**: 33 *b*   **Courtesy the artist and Metro Pictures, New York**: 110 *l*   **Photo Oronoz**: 39 *l & r*, 41 *l & r*   **Fototeca Instituto Nacional de Antropologia e Historia, Pachuca, Mexico**/photo © Nacho Lopez: 98 *br*   **Museo Nacional, La Paz**: 32, 93   **Private collection, La Paz**: 91, 92 *c*   **Courtesy Office de Tourisme, Le Puy-en-Velay**: 38 *iv*   **Icon Museum, Recklinghausen**: 33 *c*   **Robert Harding Picture Library**: 4–5, 54, 61, 99 *b* (Photo © Robert Frerck), 59, 60, 75 *r* (Photo © Christopher Rennie), 107 (Photo © Liam White), 109*a* (Photo © Explorer) *& cl*   **Photo Rodrigo Rojas**: 88 *al*   **San Clemente, Rome**: 15   **Photo © Janusz Rosikoń**: 8, 9, 20, 21, 22, 24–25, 27, 69 *br*   **Photo © Dana Salvo**: 98 *a*, 99 *al*   **Photo © Chloë Sayer**: 102 *al*

Photo Scala/Museo Nazionale, Napoli: 13 *bl*   **Photo Sea and See, Paris**: 11, 63*r*, 71, 76–77, 102 *bl*   **By permission of Basilica de la Macarena, Seville**: 6   **Courtesy Secretariado de Publicaciones, Universidad de Sevilla**: 64   **Monastery of St Catherine, Sinai**: 16 *l*   **Photo © James Sparshatt**: 67 *a*, 74 *a*   **Photo Ivan Terestchenko**: 51 *ar*, 68, 102 *l*, 103 *l*, 106 *al & bl*   **Tesoro Cathedral, Toledo**: 67 *cl*   **Photo Jean-Claude Toulouse**: 30   **Courtesy Dominique Mazeaud, Photo Kay Turner**: 3   **Musei Vaticani**: 13 *br*

Above: Our Lady of the Snows, a modern plaster Virgin.